TRADEMARK DESIGNS OF THE WORLD

by Yusaku Kamekura

With a Preface by Paul Rand

DOVER PUBLICATIONS, INC., NEW YORK

This Dover edition, first published in 1981, is a reprint of the work originally published circa 1975 by George Wittenborn, Inc., New York, and David Publishing Co., Ltd, Tokyo, under the title *Trademarks of the World*. All the trademark designs from the original edition are included in this reprint, but a brief introductory essay on Japanese crests has been deleted.

International Standard Book Number: 0-486-24191-2
Library of Congress Catalog Card Number: 81-66711

Manufactured in the United States of America
Dover Publications, Inc.
180 Varick Street
New York, N. Y. 10014

PREFACE

Like many Westerners, my admiration for Japanese art and architecture has led me to study the subject with enthusiasm. The influence of Japanese art on western art is a fact western designers and artists readily admit. That such great artists as Lautrec, Van Gogh and Gauguin were vitally affected by the Japanese print is common knowledge. In the case of Lautrec this influence is manifested not only in the simplicity, space concept and general composition of his work, but the artist's very signature, in the form of a blazon, is evidence of his love for Japanese design.

In my own case Japanese painting, design and marks have perhaps had more influence on my work than any other single art form. And my study of Japanese art has not merely given me some understanding of Oriental art but it has increased my understanding of modern western painting and design. This may appear a strange remark, but I recall my days in grammar school when it was impossible for me to understand English grammar until I had studied a foreign language.

To many it would seem strange that the Japanese commercial artist should now be influenced by the West, the Bauhaus, western typography and western trademarks. Yet, on closer examination it is not at all strange. The Japanese artist has merely rediscovered something familiar, something he has always known, something having perhaps a slightly different physiognomy, but nevertheless an old friend. This is the Japanese way of thinking a simple, concentrated and direct language.

Because of this the Japanese artist is particularly well equipped to design trademarks. The trademark, being both form and substance, both idea as well as picture, is one of the most challenging problems for a designer—its solution must be of the utmost simplicity. The Japanese alphabet (ideographs) and Japanese family blazons are perfect models for trademarks as we know them today.

In commerce the trademark is a language understood by all. It can traverse national boundaries and is as intelligible to an American as it is to a Japanese. In its small way, the trademark demonstrates the possibilities not only of a universal language but, more important, of universal understanding.

PAUL RAND

INTRODUCTION

Durable and aesthetic trademarks are of great commercial value today because they symbolize the aims and activities of an organization. An effective symbol is an excellent sales agent for, though a person may not remember the name of a company, he will recognize and buy from its mark.

For many years the trademarks of Europe and America have not only promoted products but enhanced their appearance, and now Japan is reaching this refined and integrated stage. However, selecting a good symbol is not easy and most of the popular methods used in Japan have been rather unsuccessful.

Some organizations ask their employees for suggestions and take the best idea submitted. For example, one company decided on a clumsy variation of the Ford symbol, but such an imitation lacks the originality and uniqueness necessary to survive. The contest method is also unreliable as most of the entries are usually random ideas and designs based on current fashions or fads. A mark chosen from this group, though popular for a while, would gradually lose its strength and beauty and soon be labeled, as the old Japanese proverb states, "a useless treasure."

Sometimes the chief executive asks a number of outstanding artists to submit their designs, and then he selects the best one from the collected group. However, this superior system is ruined if that top executive in turn submits the candidate's mark to a board of directors who fail to appreciate the distinctive and spontaneous qualities of the design and demand certain deadening and dulling changes. They may have fixed ideas as to what their company stands for, which is fine, but such attitudes may restrict the artist's creativity. Of course the good designer should know the company and its product in order to create a related design which will promote the merchandise, but, in turn, he must be allowed the artistic freedom necessary to keep his work from becoming stiff and lifeless.

Once Japanese manufacturers realize that a worthy design can be produced by a sensitive and well-informed artist and learn to distinguish the versatile design from the well-proportioned form, more and more valuable trademarks will begin to appear.

After a trademark has been selected, it must be tended. It must be kept fresh and alive. However, most businessmen become sentimentally attached to their marks and are reluctant to change that which has seen them through many hardships as well as successes. If these men stubbornly stick to the old and are unwilling to modify and modernize, their beloved symbols will no longer appeal to the public.

About fifty years ago the trademark of the Japanese company Fukusuke Tabi (sock manufacturers) showed an old Japanese mascot. This theme has gradually been rejuvenated and transformed into a young smiling face. Even the original angel symbol of the Morinaga Confectionery Company, one of the largest candy and foodstuff manufacturers in Japan, has changed considerably since its adoption. As an extreme example, the well-known symbol of the Milan "Triennale" exhibition of industrial arts is dramatically altered for each session by a renowned designer.

There is no doubt that the selection and care of a good trademark requires a great deal of time and effort. However, the reward lies in a result which possesses a durable and flexible combination of artistic and commercial qualities.

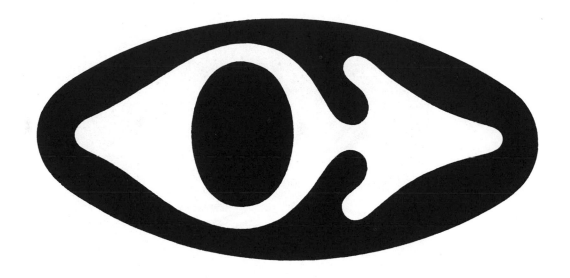

1

2

3

4

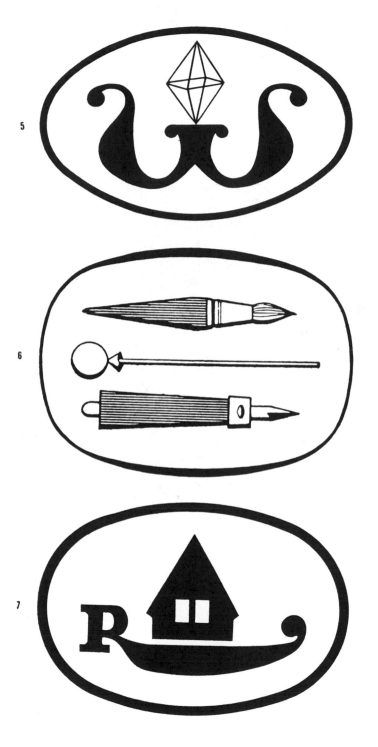

8

9

10

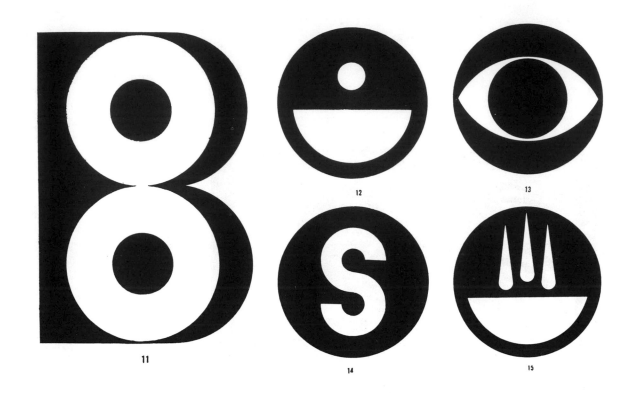

11

12

13

14

15

16

17
18
19
20
21
22

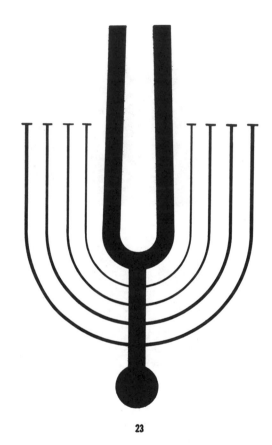

23

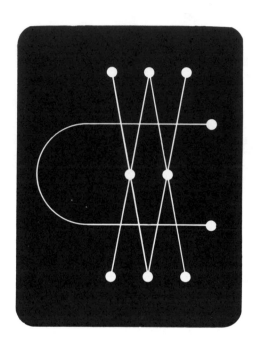

24

25

26

27

28

29

DIE SONNE VON ST. MORITZ
IL SOLE DI ST. MORITZ
THE SUN OF ST. MORITZ
LE SOLEIL DE ST. MORITZ

30

GUILDE DU VIN

31

HAUCK · WIEN
WIENER · LIKÖRE

32

17

33

34

35

36

37

38

39

40

41

42

45

48

43

46

49

44

47

50

51

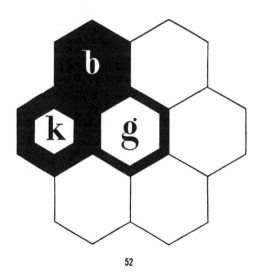

52

53

54

55

56

57

58

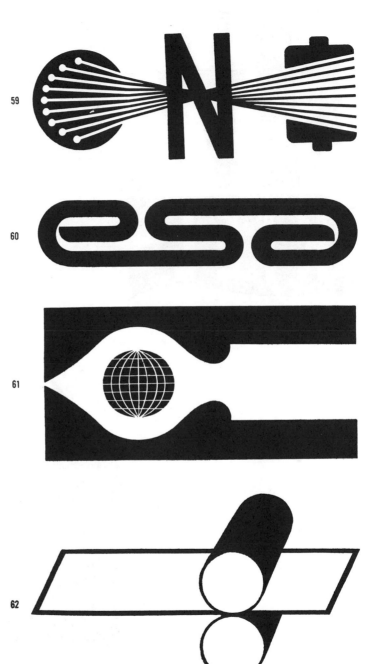

59

60

61

62

63

64

28

65

66

67

68

69

70

71

72

73

74

75

76

77   78   79   80   81

82   83   84   85   86

87

88

89

90

91

92

95

96

97

100

101

102

93

94

98

99

103

104

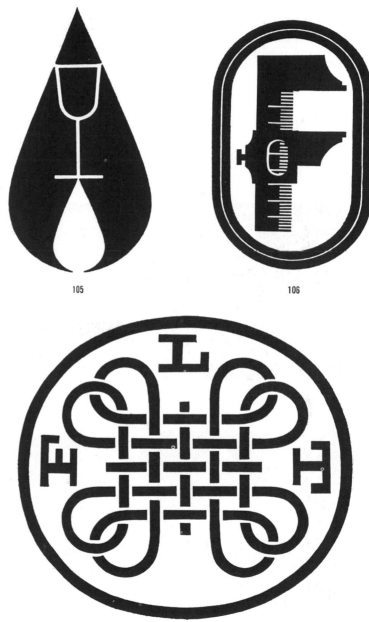

105

106

107

108

109

112

110

111

113

114

115

116

117

118

119

120

121

122

123

124

125

126

127

128

129   130   131   132

138   139   140   141

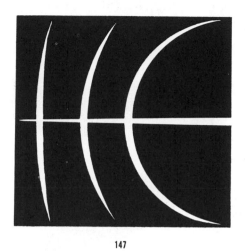

147

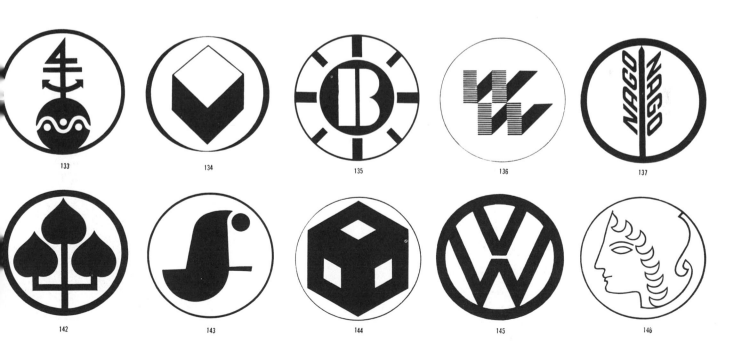

133

134

135

136

137

142

143

144

145

146

148

150

149

151

39

152

153

154

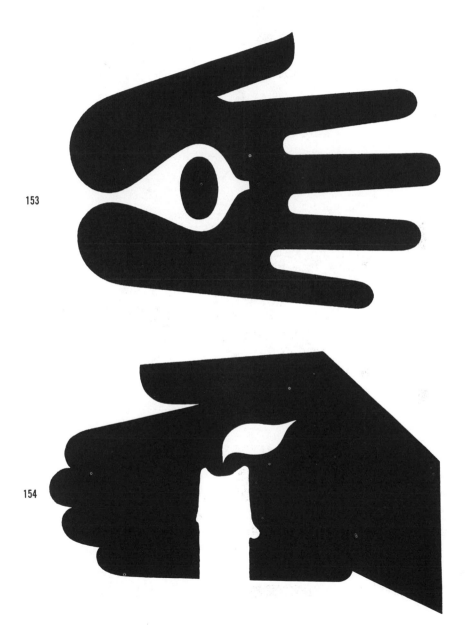

155

156

157

158

159

160

164

161

162

163

165

166

167

168

169

170

174

171

172

173

43

PUBLICITÉ

175

176

177

178

179

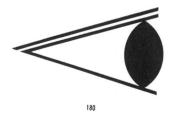

180

181

182

183

184

185

186

187

188

189

KNORR 190

KORN 191

192

ERIC NASMITH 193

Caribe Hilton

194

CARSTEN

197

198

199

195

196

200

47

201

202

203

204

205

207

208

209

210

211

213

214

215

216

217

206

212

218

219

220

221

222

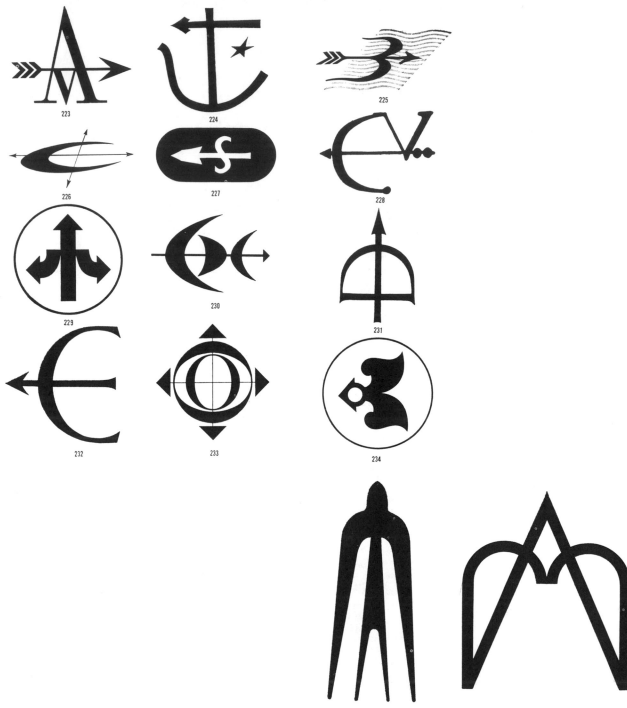

223

224

225

226

227

228

229

230

231

232

233

234

235

236

237

238

239

240

241

242

53

Liberty

243

244

245

246

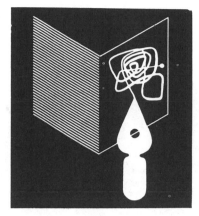

247

248

249

251

250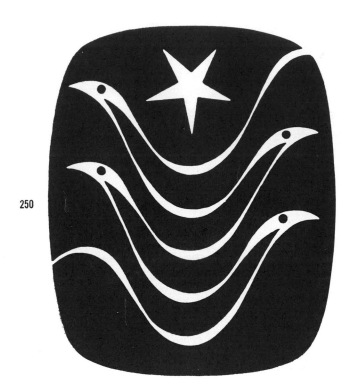

252

253

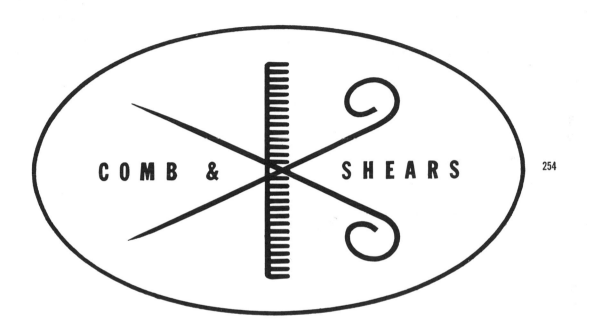

COMB & SHEARS 254

255

256

257

258

259

260

261

262

263

264

265

60

266

267   268   269   270

271   272   273   274

61

275

277

278

279

280

281

282

283

284

276

285

286

287

288

289

290

291

292

293

294

295

296

297

298

299

300

301

302

303

304

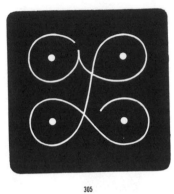

305

306

307

308

309

310

311

312

313

314

315

316

317

318

319

320

321

322

323

69

324

325

328

329

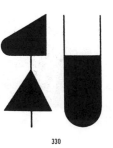

330

331

332

326

327

333

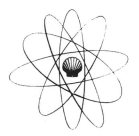

334

335

336

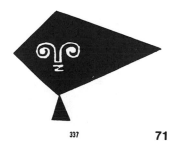

337

338

339

340

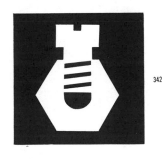

341

342

343

344

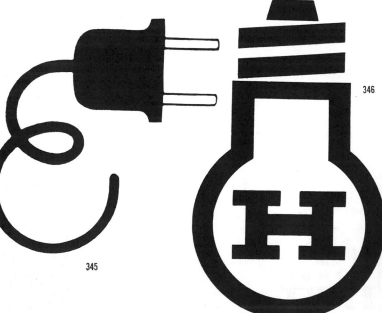

345

346

347

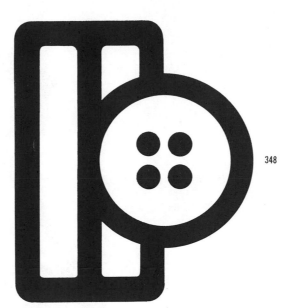

348

349

350

351

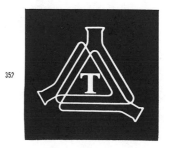

352

353

354

355

356

SAGITTAIRE

357

358

359

360

361

362

363

365

366

367

368

369

370

364

371

372

373

374

375

376

377

378

379

78

380

381

382

383

385

386

384

388

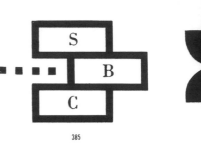

389

390

391

VETR O FLEX

387

392 ITY DRUCK

393 VVV

TESA

394

OERLIKON

embru

395

+GF+

396

397

83

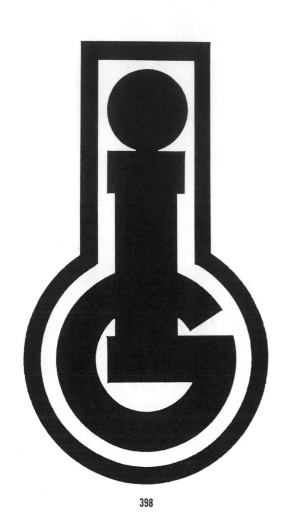

398

399

400

401

402

403

404

405

406

407

408

409

410

411

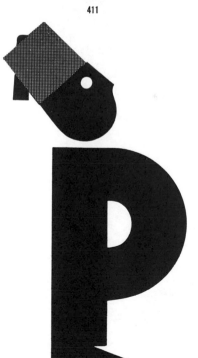

412

413

414

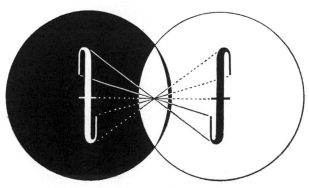

415

416

417

420

418

421

419

422

87

423

424

425

427

426

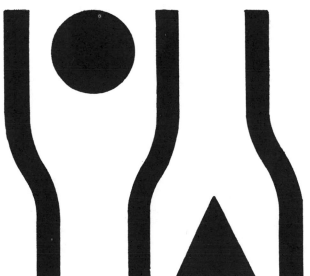

428

429

430

431

432

433

434

435

436

437

438

439

440

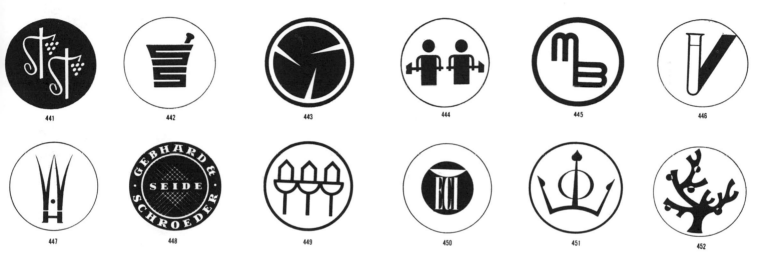

441　　　　442　　　　443　　　　444　　　　445　　　　446

447　　　　448　　　　449　　　　450　　　　451　　　　452

SEIDE

GEBHARD & SCHROEDER

455

456

453

454

457

459

461

458

460

462

463

464

465

466

467

468

469

470

471

472

473

474

475

476

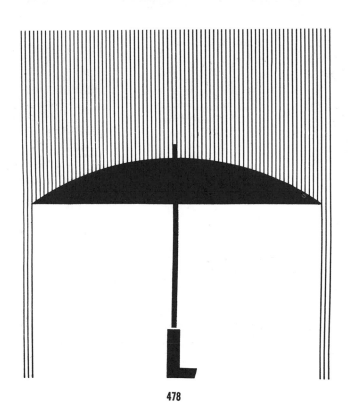

478

477

479

480

481

482

483

484

485

486

487

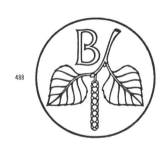
488

489

490

491

492

493

494

495

496

500

501

502

503

497

498

499

504

505

506

507

508

509

510

511

514

515

516

517

518

519

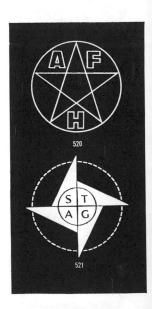

520

521

512

513

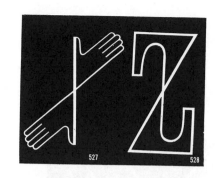

527

528

522

523

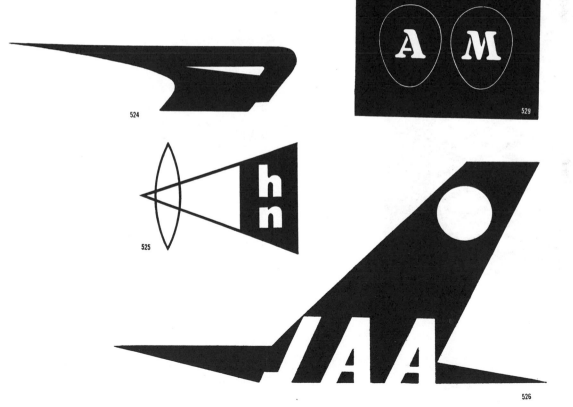

524

525

529

526

530

531

532

533

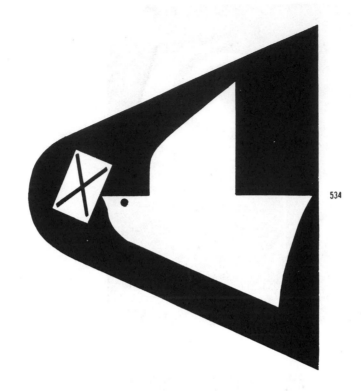

534

535

536

537

538

539

540

541

542

543

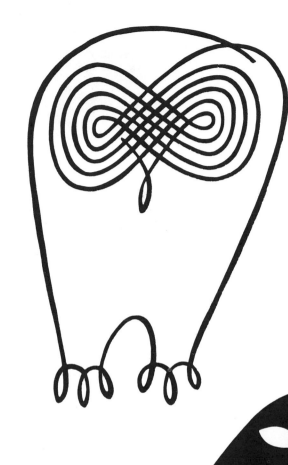

544

545

546

547

548

549

550

551

552

553

554

555

556

557

558

559

560

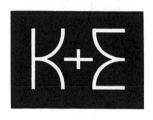

561

562

563

564

565

111

566

570

567

ERNST

568

569

571

572

573

574

575

576

577

578

579

580

581

586

587

588

589

590

582

583

585

584

591

592

593

594

115

595

596

599

597

601

602

598

603

604

600

605

606

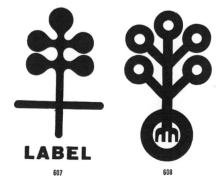

LABEL

607

608

609

610

611

612

613

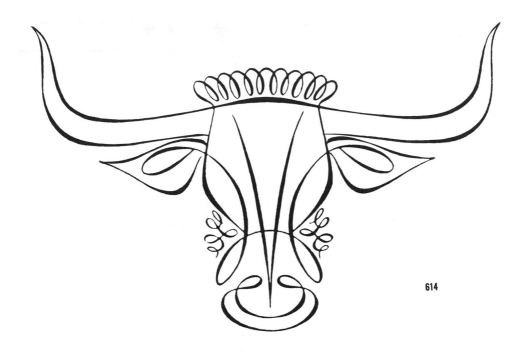

614

615

119

616

617

618

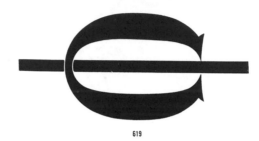

619

620

621

622

623

624

625

627

628

629

630

631

626

632

633

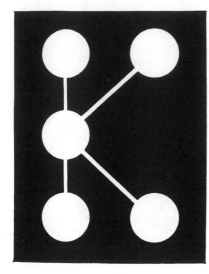

634

635

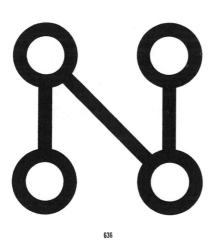

636

637

124

638

639

640

641

645

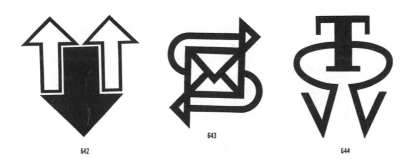

642

643

644

646

647

648

649

650

651

652

653

657

654

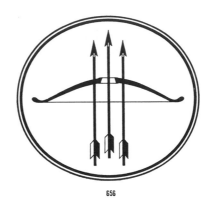

656

658

655

659

660

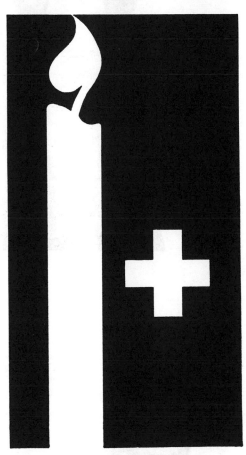

661

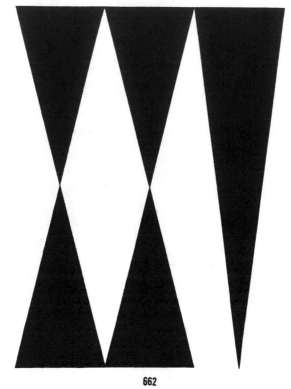

662

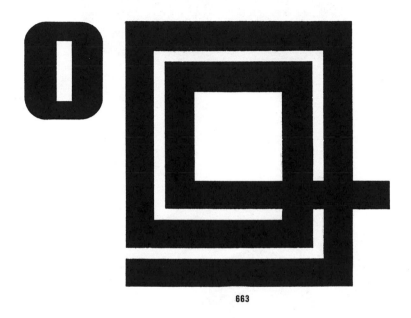

663

664

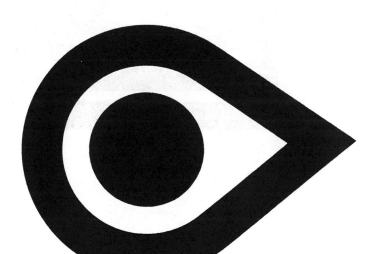

665

666

667

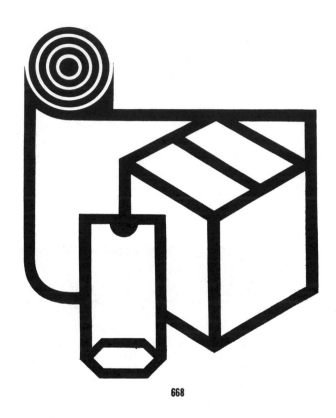

668

669

670

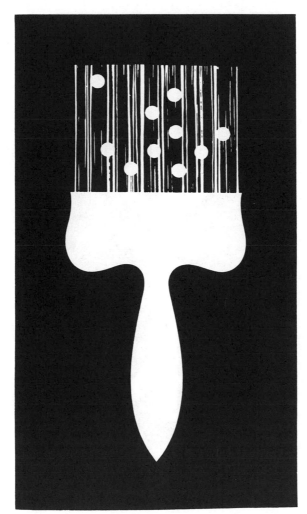

671

672

673

674

675

676

677

678

679

680

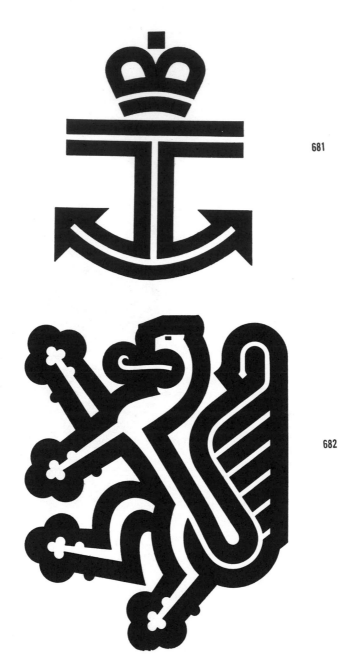

681

682

683

684

685

686

143

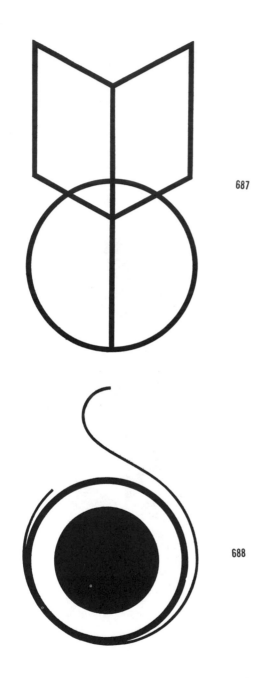

687

688

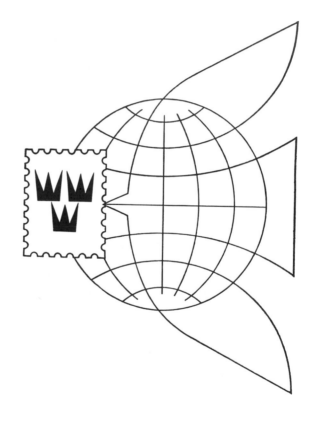

689

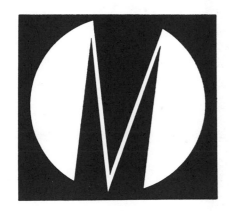

690

691

692

693

694

695

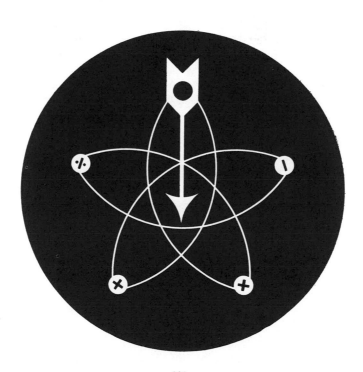

696

697

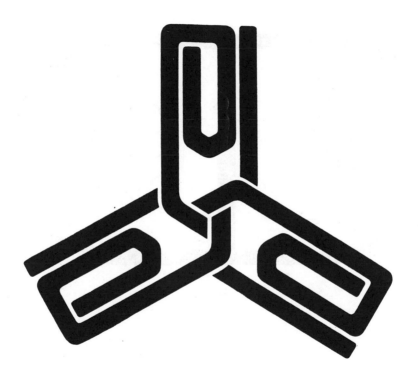

698

699

BIBLIOGRAPHY

BOOKS

SCHWEIZER SIGNETE	*(Amstutz & Herdeg, GRAPHIS PRESS, Zurich. 1948)*
TRADEMARK DESIGN	*(Paul Theobald, Publisher, Chicago. 1952)*
GRAPHIS ANNUAL	*(Amstutz & Herdeg, GRAPHIS PRESS, Zurich)*
MODERN PUBLICITY	*(The Studio Publications, London)*
PUBLICITÉ	*(Maurice Collet, Editeur, Geneva)*
PUBBLICITÀ IN ITALIA	*(Editrice l'Ufficio Moderno, Milan)*
DESIGNERS IN BRITAIN	*(Allan Wingate, London)*

MAGAZINES

GRAPHIS	*(Amstutz & Herdeg, GRAPHIS PRESS, Zurich)*
GEBRAUCHSGRAPHIK	*(Verlag F. Bruckmann KG, Munich)*
PUBLIMONDIAL	*(Edi-Mondial, Paris)*
GRAPHIK	*(Verlag Maiwald, Stuttgart)*
ART & INDUSTRY	*(The Studio Publications, London)*
STILE INDUSTRIA	*(Istituto Editoriale Domus, Milan)*
INDUSTRIAL DESIGN	*(Whitney Publications Inc., New York)*
IDEA	*(Seibundo-Shinkosha Publishing Co., Ltd., Tokyo)*
PORTFOLIO	*(Zebra Press, Cincinnati)*

IDENTIFICATION OF MARKS
ILLUSTRATED

I have spent much time and made many enquiries in my efforts to make the data furnished as correct as possible. Unfortunately in a number of cases I received no reply and, as a result, the names of the author, country and company often remain in doubt or unknown. The trademarks are identified in the following form:

Designer (Country) Company or Type of Organization

1   Walther Bergmann (Germany) Odyssee Angel Publishing Co.
2   Louis Danziger (USA) General Lighting Co.
3   Paul Rand (USA) Helbros Watch Co.
4   Herbert Leupin (Switzerland) Screw Manufacturer
5   Yusaku Kamekura (Japan) Wako Department Store
6   Geo. Mayhew (England) Sign & Display Union
7   Hans Renner (Germany)
8   R. A. Hetze (Germany) Gunsch Glass Instrument Works
9   Willi Bahner (Austria) Bibliotheca Bibliographica
10 Jobst Kuch (?   ) Andrea Seed Co.
11 Heinrich Wehmeier (Germany) Printers
12 Clar-Werbung (Germany) Saccharin Manufacturer
13 Morton Goldsholl (USA) CBS Television
14 Ladislav Sutnar (USA) Sweet File Co.
15 Joseph Binder (Germany) Fissan Milk Co.
16 Hans Schleger (England) Helois Printing Co.
17 Joseph Binder (Germany) United Printing Co.
18 Hiroshi Ohchi (Japan) Goo Institute of Organic Chemistry
19 Walter Sauer (Germany) Seed Wholesaler
20 Walter Sauer (Germany)
21 Max & Eugen Lenz (Switzerland) Switzerland's European Relief Work
22 Hans Hartmann (Switzerland) Switzerland's Carpenters Union
23 Werner Epstein (Israel) Orchestra
24 Alvin Lustig (USA)
25 Robert Sessler (Switzerland) Schaffhaus Cotton-Wool Co.
26 Carlo Vivarelli (Italy) Twist Drill Works
27 Joseph Binder (Germany) Montreal Fishing Co.
28 Jupp Ernst (Germany) Gaerres Co.
29 Jupp Ernst (Germany)
30 Walter Herdeg (Switzerland) Symbol for St. Moritz
31 Ch. Kuhn (Switzerland) Wine Guild

32 Hans Gaensslen (Austria) Wiener Liquor Firm
33 Honegger-Lavater (Switzerland)
34–35 Honegger-Lavater (Switzerland) Bauer Hotel
36 Hermann Eidenbenz (Switzerland) Renbolt & Christie Carrosserie Co.
37 Walter Leonhalt (Germany)
38 Hiroshi Ohchi (Japan) Ichioka Pharmacy
39 Heiner Zinckgraf (Germany)
40 Errel (Israel) Government of Israel
41 Meier Menzel/Gatz (Germany)
42 Meier Menzel/Gatz (Germany) Chocolate Manufacturer
43 Meier Menzel/Gatz (Germany) Lock Manufacturer
44 Meier Menzel/Gatz (Germany)
45 Meier Menzel/Gatz (Germany)
46 Meier Menzel/Gatz (Germany) Cadbury's Chocolate
47 Meier Menzel/Gatz (Germany)
48 Meier Menzel/Gatz (Germany)
49 Meier Menzel/Gatz (Germany) Lock Manufacturer
50 Meier Menzel/Gatz (Germany) House Builders
51 Goetz Neuke (Germany)
52 Hermann Eidenbenz (Switzerland) Cultural Society
53 Unidentified
54 Charles Dean (USA) Busy Bee Candy Line
55 Bruno Munari (Italy) Symbol for Tenth Triennale of Milan
56 Jacques Nathan (France) Symbol for a Convention
57 Max Koerner (Germany) Plate-Glass Manufacturer
58 Walter Herdeg (Switzerland) Furniture Manufacturer
59 Walther Bergmann (Germany)
60 Hans Hartmann (Switzerland) ESA Marketing Assoc. of the Swiss Motor Trade
61 Jupp Ernst (Germany) Symbol for the International Exhibition of Canadian Commercial Art
62 Tom Schell (?   ) Aluminum Rolling Mill
63 E. R. Vogenauer (Germany) Symbol for Kiel Week
64 L. de Miranda (Denmark) Building Society
65 Hans Schleger (England) Mac Fisheries Co.
66 Joseph Autherid (Austria)
67 Max Koerner (Switzerland) Wolf & Son
68 W. Weiskoening (Switzerland) Eternum Co.

69 (Switzerland) J. R. Geigy Pharmaceutical Manufacturer
70 Dr. Hahn (Germany) Tourist Office
71 Duda/Tyfa/Misek (Czechoslovakia) Lenka Textile Manufacturer
72 Honegger-Lavater (Switzerland) Artificial Fertilizer Manufacturer
73 Heiner Zinckgraf (Germany)
74 P. Wenger (Switzerland) Emil Maechler Furniture Co.
75 S. Blickman
76 Heinrich Steding (Germany)
77 (Germany)
78 Ernst Paar (Austria)
79 Karl Heinz Dellbrugge (Germany)
80 Tadashi Ohmi (Japan) Aoki Printing Co.
81 Heiner Zinckgraf (Germany)
82 Robert S. Gessner (Switzerland) Hobby Society
83 Joseph Binder (Germany) Dornes Co.
84 Erwin Krubeck (Germany) Sailors' Mission
85 Shichiro Imatake (Japan) Kansaï Organic Chemistry Co.
86 Herbert Stengel (Germany)
87 (Switzerland) Switzerland Industrial Exhibition
88 Pierre Gauchat (Switzerland) Rope Manufacturer
89 Walter Herdeg (Switzerland) Interior Decorator's Sign
90 Fritz Helinger (Switzerland) Cold Storage Depot
91 W. Bruderer (Switzerland)
92 Gerd Leufelt (Germany) Symbol for a Kindergarten
93 Walter Bergmann (Germany)
94 Tadashi Ohashi (Japan) Restaurant
95 Donald Brun (Switzerland) F. Bluemer & Co.
96 Hans Gaensslen (Germany)
97 Hermann Virl (Germany)
98 Dr. Hahn (Germany) Campaign for Utilization of Forest Plants
99 (USA) Lighting Equipment Company
100 Honegger-Lavater (Switzerland) Swiss Bank Association
101 F. Afflerbach (Switzerland)
102 Josef Autherid (Austria)
103 Morihiko Iwamoto (Japan) Sanko-Sha Advertising Agency
104 Willy Simmler (?   ) Stationery
105 Franz Hermann Wills (Germany) Liquor Firm

106 Albert Ruegg (Switzerland) Machine Workshops
107 Kurt Wills (?   ) Hemp Manufacturer
108 Honegger-Lavater (Switzerland) Travel Agency
109 Walter Sauer (Germany)
110 Max Koerner (Germany) Chocolate Co.
111 Hans Ernst (?   ) Woolen Yarn Co.
112 Isa Hesse (Switzerland) Sports & Travel Equipment Firm
113 Goetz Neucke (Germany)
114 Goetz Neucke (Germany)
115 Alfons Grimm (Switzerland) Swansdown Co.
116 Gerhard Kreische (Germany) Fowlers
117 Leo Pernitsche (Austria)
118 Josef Autherid (Austria)
119 Ernst Boehm (Germany)
120 F. Stapel (Denmark) Copper Manufacturer
121 Dr. Hahn (Germany) Advertising Agency
122 Josef Autherid (Austria)
123 Ludwig Winter
124 Walther Bergmann (Germany)
125 Yasuhiro Kojima (Japan) Tanita Works
126 Carlo Vivarelli (Switzerland) Linoleum Firm
127 K. Sieth (Germany)
128 Walter Sauer (Switzerland) Instrument Co.
129 Unidentified
130–132 Goetz Neucke (Germany)
133 Josef Tyfa (Czechoslovakia) Handkerchief Manufacturer
134 Heinz Schwabe (Germany) Publishing House
135 Walter Leonhard (Germany)
136 Hans/Ruth Albitz (Germany)
137 Albert Ruegg (Switzerland) Nago Food Products Company
138 Heinrich Steding (Germany)
139 (Switzerland)
140 Joseph Binder (Germany) Chemical Manufacturer
141 Unidentified
142 G. F. Schmidt (?   ) Manufacturer of Pharmaceutical Products
143 Willi Harnischmacher
144 Goetz Neucke (Germany)
145 (Germany) Volkswagen Automobile Co.

246 Paul Rand (USA) Robeson Cutlery Co.
247 Morton Goldsholl (USA) Paul Theobald Publishing Co.
248 Paul Rand (USA) Gibson Diamond Co.
249 George Tscherny (USA) Whitney Publications Inc.
250 Franz Hermann Wills (Germany) Bird's Paradise on the North Sea
251 Kenji Ito (Japan) Wako Department Store
252 Dr. Hahn (Germany) Publishing House
253 Felix Mueller & K. O. Blase (Switzerland)
254 Alvin Lustig (USA) Barber's Materials
255-264 Goetz Neucke (Germany)
265 Dr. Hahn (Germany) Shop of Dolls in National Costumes
266 Jacques Nathan (France) Piece Goods Firm
267 Walther Bergmann (Germany)
268 Dr. Hahn (Germany) Spice and Foodstuff Manufacturer
269 Dr. Hahn (Germany) Chair Manufacturer
270 P. Haase (Germany)
271 P. Zuerrer (Switzerland) Carpenter
272 Philipp Seitz (Switzerland) Wine Wholesaler
273 Philipp Seitz (Switzerland) Tea Importer
274 Dr. Hahn (Germany) Printing House
275 Herbert Bayer (USA) Mark of Aspen
276 George Nelson (USA) Herman Miller Furniture Co.
277 Ezio Bonini (Italy) Pirelli Rubber Co.
278 H. Eidenbenz (Switzerland) Hans Wullschleger
279 Eugen & Max Lenz (Switzerland) Bookbinder's Shop
280 Karl Langenbacher (Germany) Schneck Oil Co.
281 Paul Rand (USA) John David Stores
282 W. Diethelm (Switzerland) Cellux Agricultural Machinery Co.
283 (Germany) Lorenz Radio
284 Hubert Troost (Germany)
285 Yusaku Kamekura (Japan) Japan Industrial Designers Association
286 Eugen & Max Lenz (Switzerland) Banziger Publishing Co.
287 (England) The Phaidon Press
288 Heinlich Wehmeier (Germany) August Bagel Publishing Co.
289 W. Kach (Switzerland) Buhl Publishing Co.
290 Etienne Bucher (France) Gardeners
291 Peter Wolbrand (Germany)
292 Tobias Schwab
293 Hans Moehling
294 Shigemi Hijikata (Japan) Japan Cinema Industry Labor Union
295 Hans Moehling
296 Hans Thoeni (Switzerland) Swiss Association of Civil Engineers & Architects
297 W. Diethelm (Switzerland) H. Haeusler & Co.
298 J. O. Reinecke (USA) Motorola Electronic Apparatus Co.
299 Takashi Kono (Japan) Japan Advertising Artists Club
300 Max Huber (Switzerland) Metal Manufacturer
301 Yusaku Kamekura (Japan) Musashino City Planning Co.

302 Minoru Deushi (Japan) Tokyo Commercial Artists Association
303 Hans Hartmann (Switzerland) Stone Quarriers
304 Paul Rand (USA) Smith, Kline & French Laboratory
305 Alvin Lustig (USA) Motion Picture Co.
306 Josef Autherid (Austria)
307 E. R. Vogenauer (Germany)
308 Josef Autherid (Austria)
309 Hiromu Hara (Japan) National Museum of Modern Art
310 Ervin Krubeck (Germany) Fruit Importers
311 Gerhard Kreische (Germany)
312 Gerd Leufert (Germany) Rhein-Main-Donau Shipping Co.
313 Paul Sollberger (Switzerland) Rhone-Rhein Shipping Co.
314 Hermann Eidenbenz (Switzerland) Trading Co.
315 Gerhard Kreische (Germany) Sailing Association of Berlin
316 Gerhard Kreische (Germany) Sailing Association of Berlin
317 (Australia) QANTAS Empire Airways
318 Walther Bergmann (Germany)
319 Eugen & Max Lenz (Switzerland) Legler Textile Co.
320 Karl Brocken (USA) Airline Co.
321 (Switzerland) Swissair
322 Hans Schleger (England) Waterproof Cloth Co.
323 Kurt Tillessen (Germany)
324 Wolf D. Zimmermann (Germany) Symbol of a Library
325 Hans Hartmann (Switzerland) Sports Equipment Shop
326 John Ciampi (England) Shoe Store
327 Paul Achwanden (Switzerland) Gear Manufacturer
328 Unidentified
329 John Ciampi (England) Publishing House
330 Hiroshi Ohchi (Japan) Wako Department Store
331 Kenneth Bromfield (England) Central Council for Health Education
332 Hans Hartmann (Switzerland) Scaffolding Constructor
333 Jacques Nathan (France) Milk Products Co.
334 E. R. Aspinall (England) Shell-Mex Co.
335 Ryuichi Yamashiro (Japan) Publishing House
336 Hans Schleger (England) Cattle Remedy
337 Tadashi Ohashi (Japan) Shampoo Manufacturer
338 Alfons Grimm (Switzerland) Bakery
339 Philipp Seitz (Switzerland) Musical Instruments Store
340 Lucian Bernhard (Germany) Coffee Roasting Establishment
341 P. Zuerrer (Switzerland) Drug Store
342 Hermann Bentele (Germany)
343 Fore (France) Publishing House
344 Boehme (Germany) Electric Goods Co.
345 Dr. Hahn (Germany) Electrical Appliances Manufacturer
346 Joseph Binder (Germany) Electrical Instruments Manufacturer
347 Joseph Binder (Germany) Insurance Co.
348 Josef Autherid (Austria) Piece Goods Store
349 John Maas (USA) Chemical Manufacturer
350 Walter Leonhard (Germany)

445 Paul Helms (Germany)
446 Dr. Hahn (Germany) Chemical Works
447 Hiromu Hara (Japan) Wako Department Store
448 Sigmund von Weech (Germany) Silk Co.
449 (Germany) Printing House
450 H. A. Rothholz (Ceylon) Eastern Chemical Industries Co.
451 Ayao Yamana (Japan) Sun Pharmaceutical Co.
452 Joseph Binder (Germany) Koralle Co.
453 Wich (Germany) Publishing House
454 Milner Gray (England) Beer Brewery
455 Artists' Society of Darmstadt
456 Hans Hartmann (Switzerland) Chalk Supplier
457 Pierre Comte (France) Publishing House
458 E. R. Vogenauer (Germany) Publishing House
459 Jean Picart le Doux (France)
460 Charles Dean (USA) Confectionery
461 (Germany)
462 Adolf Flueckiger (Switzerland) Symbol for a Swiss Gastronomy Exhibition
463 David Stone Martin (USA) Norman Grants & His JATP Jazz Orchestra
464 Hermann Bentele (Germany) Clothing Manufacturer
465 Helmut Kurtz (Switzerland) Swiss Central Office for Aid & Refugees
466 Albe Steiner (Italy) Linoleum Firm
467 (Switzerland) Publishing House
468 Franz Hermann Wills (Germany) Instrument Makers
469 Hermann Bentele (Germany)
470 F. H. K. Henrion (England)
471 Albe Steiner (Italy) La Rinascente, a Department Store
472 Franz F. H. Wagner (Germany)
473 Hans Kasser (Switzerland) Precision Engineering Works
474 Rudolf Koch (Germany) Symbol of a Religious Circle
475 Takashi Kono (Japan) Wako Department Store
476 Hans Hartmann (Switzerland) Architect's Sign
477 Dr. Hahn (Germany) Cosmetics Manufacturer
478 Dr. Hahn (Germany) Umbrella Manufacturer
479 Koodin Lapow Association (?) I. Rokeach & Sons
480 Ruth Dorland (Germany) Publishing House
481 Holabird & Root & Burgee (USA) Intercontinental Hotels Co.
482 Hermann Eidenbenz (Switzerland) Pharmaceutical Manufacturer
483 Albert Ruegg (Switzerland) Bookbinder
484 Raymond Loewy Associates (USA) Ekco Products Co.
485 H. Hauser (Switzerland) René Allemand
486 Anton Stankowski (Germany) International Exhibition of German Handicrafts
487 Gerhard Kreische (Germany) A Book Emblem
488 Jan Tschichold (Switzerland) Publisher's Colophon
489 Milner Gray (England) Pyrex Products

490 Walther Bergmann (Germany) Signet of the Artist
491 E. R. Vogenauer (Germany) Contractor
492 Alfred Mahlan (Germany) Flour Mill
493 George Salter (USA) Tower Books
494 (Germany)
495 P. Pickard Jenkins (England) National Cash Register Co., Ltd.
496 Honegger-Lavater (Switzerland) Bank
497 Heinz Lauscher (Germany)
498 Eric Frazer (England) Symbol for London Mystery Magazine
499 W. Kach (Switzerland) Mark of Zurich
500 Hans Hartmann (Switzerland) Office Equipment
501 Hermann Eidenbenz (Switzerland) Emblem of Basel
502 Hans Hartmann (Switzerland) Sport Equipment Co.
503 Hermann Eidenbenz (Switzerland) Emblem of Zurich
504 Carlo Vivarelli (Switzerland) Neri Drug Store
505 (Switzerland) International Watch Co.
506 Frank Riley (USA) Tube Turns Inc.
507 Raymond Loewy Associates (USA) International Harvester Co.
508 Ayao Yamana (Japan) Wako Department Store
509 Walter Kaech (Switzerland) Textile Manufacturer
510 Paul Sollberger (Switzerland) Air Conditioning Plant Equipment Co.
511 Walter Sauer (Germany) Spinning Co.
512 Duda/Tyfa/Misek (Czechoslovakia) Builder
513 Heinrich Steding (Germany)
514 Joseph Binder (Germany) Chemical Industry Co.
515 National Tile Co.
516 Hans Hartmann (Switzerland) Swiss Fruit Growers & Distributors
517 Heinz Schwabe (Germany) Party Badge
518 Goetz Neucke (Germany)
519 Dr. A. Heritier (Switzerland) Binaca Co.
520 Hans Neuburg (Switzerland) Electric Machinery
521 Karl Hans Walter (Germany) Exhibition Symbol
522 (Austria) A. B. Dick Co.
523 Dr. Hahn (Germany) Cardboard Factory
524 Eberhard Thunert (Germany)
525 Carl Dair (Canada) Herb Natt & Co.
526 Takashi Kohno (Japan) Japan Air Association
527 W. Hoelter (Germany)
528 H. A. Albitz & R. Albitz (Germany)
529 Kenneth Bromfield (England) Egg Co.
530 Hermann Kosel (?) Fruit Importer
531 Hermann Eidenbenz (Switzerland) Dolphin Shoes
532 Paul Rand (USA) Zebra Press
533 Kinkichi Takahashi (Japan) Rekitei Poetry Club
534 Jupp Ernst (Germany) Paper Manufacturer
535 Philipp Seitz (Germany) Lighting Equipment Co.
536 Stasa Blazkova (Czechoslovakia) Furniture & Textile Manufacturer

537 Tadashi Ohashi (Japan) Black Cat Club
538 Albert Appenzeller (Switzerland) Pharmaceutical Co.
539 Hermann Eidenbenz (Switzerland) Pharmaceutical Co.
540 Milner Gray (England) T. W. Thorpe Ltd.
541 Walther Bergmann (Germany)
542 Ernst Keller (Switzerland) Vaccine Manufacturer
543 Hiroshi Ohchi (Japan) Bag Shop
544 W. Hoelter (Germany)
545 Gerhard Kreische (Germany)
546 Milner Gray (England) Allen & Hanbury Co.
547 W. Bitner (Germany) Eugen Britting Shoe Manufacturer
548 L. de Miranda (Holland) Tobacco Manufacturer
549 Kenneth R. Hollick (England) Thos. Person & Sons Co.
550 Philipp Seitz (Germany) Publishing House
551 E. R. Vogenauer (Germany)
552 Hans Stempel (Germany)
553 Franz Helmuth Ehmcke (Germany) Sewing Needle Manufacturer
554 Jo Sinel (USA) Craftex Co.
555 Albro F. Downe (USA) Test Model Co.
556 E. R. Vogenauer (Germany) Savaron Publishing Co.
557 Jupp Ernst (Germany) Publishing House
558 Erick Ellegaard Frederiksen (Denmark) E. Borchersens Boghandel
559 (Switzerland) Geigy Pharmaceutical Co.
560 Max & Eugen Lenz (Switzerland) Butcher
561 Lucian Bernhard (Germany) Keuffel & Essen Co.
562 Herbert Spencer (England) "Common Ground"
563 Hiromu Hara (Japan) International Reportage Photographers Association
564 Josef Autherid (Austria)
565 U. Huber (Germany)
566 Robert Gessner (Switzerland) Design for Series of Zodiac Figures
567 Eugen & Max Lenz (Switzerland) Moton Co.
568 Robert Gessner (Switzerland) Grocers' Association
569 Goetz Neucke (Germany)
570 Walter Sauer (Germany) Fishers Association
571 Walter Sauer (Germany)
572 Hermann Virl (Germany)
573 Hermann Virl (Germany)
574 F. H. K. Henrion (England) Shoe Co.
575 William Metzig (USA) Deitch Brothers, Handbag Manufacturer
576 Joseph Binder (Germany) Symbol of an Exhibition
577 Joseph Binder (Germany)
578 Gerhardt & Teltow (Germany) Graphic Design Studio
579 Hermann Eidenbenz (Switzerland) Hemp Linen Co.
580 (Germany) Leather Co.
581 G. Troost (Germany) Wine Co.
582 Arthur Mergot (Switzerland) Printer's Emblem

583 Eugen & Max Lenz (Switzerland) Symbol of Swiss Rifle Competition
584 Hans Moller (USA) Welfare Association of America
585 Destrée (France) Blood Transfusion Service
586 Philipp Seitz (Germany) Wine Merchant
587 Tobias Schwab (?   ) Mining Co.
588 Gerhard Marx (Germany)
589 Hermann Virl (Germany)
590 Hans Moller (USA) Restaurant
591 A. Stocker
592 Joseph Binder (Germany)
593 Walter Brecker (Germany)
594 Joseph Binder (Germany) Leather Co.
595 Gerd Leufert (Germany) Printing House
596 Rudolf Froning (Germany)
597 Heinz Schwabe (Germany) Oil Mill
598 Helmut Kurtz (Switzerland) Stamp for Mill Sack
599 Robert Roser (Switzerland) Tobacco Co.
600 Walter Grieder (Switzerland) Cooperative Society of Grocery Stores
601 Heiner Zinckgraf (Germany)
602 Joseph Binder (Germany) IG Wine Distiller
603 Walter Sauer (Germany) Grossmarkt Co.
604 Hans Kasser (Switzerland) Stone Quarriers
605 Walter Brecker (Germany)
606 Gerhard Hauptmann (Germany)
607 Eugen Jordi (Switzerland) The Symbol of Fairly Paid Work
608 Paul Asal (Switzerland) Loan & Investment Trust Co.
609 Hans Schleger (England)
610 Alfred Lutz (Germany)
611 Dr. Hahn (Germany) Symbol of a Pharmacy
612 Robert Sessler (Switzerland) Road Builder
613 Paul Klee (Germany) Symbol of King and Absolute
614 Robert Sinnot (?   ) Hotel Sherman
615 Yusaku Kamekura (Japan) Symbol for a Wool Fabric
616 Raymond Loewy Associates (USA) Drum Inc.
617 (Canada) Association of Canadian Industrial Designers
618 Hermann Eidenbenz (Switzerland) Columeta Co. Ltd.
619 Unidentified
620 Herbert Matter (USA) Knoll Associates
621 H. R. Albitz (Germany)
622 Donald Brun (Switzerland)
623 F. H. K. Henrion (England)
624 F. H. K. Henrion (England)
625 Herbert Bayer (USA) Aircraft Manufacturer
626 Hermann Eidenbenz (Switzerland) Swiss Industries Fair
627 Robert Sessler (Switzerland)
628 Hans Neuburg (Switzerland) Instrument Manufacturer
629 Eugen & Max Lenz (Switzerland) Advertising Agency
630 Robert Sessler (Switzerland) Swiss Electricians Association

631 P. Zuerrer (Switzerland) Sprecher & Schuh Ltd.
632 Werner Rinke (Germany)
633 Takashi Kohno (Japan) Wako Department Store
634 Jupp Ernst (Germany) Plastics Exhibition
635 Yusaku Kamekura (Japan) Nippon Broadcasting System Inc.
636 Takashi Kohno (Japan) Japan Reportage Photographers Association
637 Robert G. Hood (USA) Arsul Chemical Co.
638 Walter Herdeg (Switzerland) Radio Gramophones
639 Robert Sessler (Switzerland) Blueprint Maker
640 Tilly Mautner (England) Rolex Paper Co. Ltd.
641 Yoshio Hayakawa (Japan) Japanese Sample Show Held in New York
642 F. H. K. Henrion (England)
643 Manfred Imbach (Switzerland) Swiss Business School
644 Kenneth Lamble (England) Trubenised Ltd.
645 Hans Schleger (England) Scandinavian Furniture Importers
646 Abram Games (England) Symbol for "Conquest of the Desert" Exhibition
647 Jupp Ernst (England) Chemical Manufacturer
648 Yoshio Hayakawa (Japan) Isora Cosmetics Co.
649 A. D. Flueckiger (Switzerland) Furniture Manufacturer
650 Manfred Imbach (Switzerland) Women's Co-operative Society
651 Walter Grieder (Switzerland) Co-operative Society
652 David Caplon (England) Symbol for Soviet Film Festival
653 Karl Prinz (Germany) Droste & Sohn Canned Beef Co.
654 Heinz Renz (Germany) Ernst Fisch Timber Co.
655 Karl Prinz (Germany) Bollmeyer Poultry Farm
656 John Buckland Wright (England) Andre Deutsch, Publisher
657 Willy Failin (Germany) Winkler Weaving Mill
658 Karl Prinz (Germany) Markische Tractor Sales Co.
659 E. H. Cuff (England) Institute for Study of Materials Handling Project
660 Gerard Miedinger (Switzerland) Bandage Manufacturer
661 Robert S. Gessner (Switzerland) Symbol for the Swiss Winter Relief Movement
662 Leo Lionni (USA) The Museum of Modern Art; Twenty-fifth Anniversary
663 Marcello Nizzoli (Italy) Olivetti Typewriter Co.
664 Waertsila-Notzjoe (Finland) Glassware Shop
665 Jupp Ernst (Germany) Business School

666 H. Waible (Italy) Peralit Co.
667 Abram Games (England) Television Service, British Broadcasting Corporation
668 Jacques Nathan (France) Central Paper Mill
669 Albe Steiner (Italy) La Rinascente
670 Marcello Nizzoli (Italy) Symbol for the 9th Triennale
671 Morton Goldsholl (USA) Paint Manufacturer
672 Takeo Yamaguchi (Japan) Art Directors' Club
673 Karl Gerstner (Switzerland) Furniture Store
674 Yusaku Kamekura (Japan) Modern Art Institute
675 Alfredo Lalia (Italy) AGIP Gas Cooperation
676 Eric Steinmueller (Argentina) Valdes & Cia.
677 Kenneth Bromfield (England) Cape Asbestos Co., Ltd.
678 Paul Froitzbein (Germany) Porsche Cars
679 Celestino Piatti (Switzerland)
680 Hansruedi Erdmann (France) Consumers Cooperative Society
681 Emil O. Biemann (Canada) Molson's Brewery Ltd.
682 Hermann Eidenbenz (Germany) Symbol of City of Braunschweig
683 Erich Unger (Germany) Hermann-Haas Office Machines Co.
684 Hiroshi Ohchi (Japan) Nichiyu Toy Co.
685 Albe Steiner (Italy) Spring Manufacturer
686 W. M. de Majo, A. Carling (England) Grayson & Co., Ltd.
687 Andreas Lerner (Germany) Reading Circle
688 Gunter Wittbold (Germany) Otto Schnug Publishing Co.
689 Martin Gavler (Sweden) Stockholm International Stamp Exhibition
690 Gottfried Honegger (Switzerland) Fruit Co-operative Union
691 Roger Geiser (Switzerland) Symbol of Review
692 Celestino Piatti (Switzerland) Public Nursery
693 Peter Schmidlin (Switzerland) Life Insurance Co.
694 Abram Games (England) Symbol for the Festival of Britain 1951
695 Saul Bass (USA) Frank Holmes Laboratories, Color Film Processors
696 F. H. K. Henrion (England) Hollerith Accounting Machines
697 G. Biilmann Petersen (Denmark) Faellestoreningen for Denmarks Brugstoreningen
698 E. & M. Lenz (Switzerland) Association of Zurich Stationery Stores
699 (USA) Heron-Teak